Good Housekeeping

D1151404

Perfect
Christmas

COLLINS & BROWN

Recipes

Lemon and Herb Roast Turkey

shopping list

- 5.4–6.3kg (12–14lb) turkey, giblets removed for Giblet Stock (*see page 25*)
- Chestnut and Butternut Squash Stuffing (*see page 6*)
- 125g (4oz) butter, softened
- 1 lemon, halved

Serves 8

Preparation Time
25 minutes

Cooking Time
4½–5 hours, plus 30 minutes resting

- 3 fresh bay leaves
- 3 fresh sage leaves
- 2 fresh rosemary sprigs
- 8 rashers rindless streaky bacon
- 350g (12oz) chipolata sausages
- salt and ground black pepper

- a bunch of mixed herbs to garnish (optional)
- **Red Wine Gravy** (*see page 7*), **Cranberry Sauce** (*see page 7*) or **Bread Sauce** (*see page 19*) to serve

How to cook

1 Take the turkey out of the refrigerator 45 minutes before stuffing it. Preheat the oven to 220°C (200°C fan oven) mark 7.

2 Put the turkey on a board and lift the neck flap. Use your fingers to ease the skin gently away from the turkey breast. Spoon in the stuffing, taking care not to overfill the cavity. Secure the flap with a cocktail stick.

3 Put a large sheet of foil in a flameproof roasting tin and put the turkey on top. Smear the turkey all over with butter, then squeeze over the lemon juice.

4 Put the squeezed lemon halves and bay leaves inside the turkey, with a sage leaf and a sprig of rosemary, then snip over the remaining sage and rosemary. Season with salt and pepper.

5 Tie the turkey legs together with string. Bring the foil over the turkey and crimp the edges together, making sure there's plenty of space between the bird and the foil. Roast for 30 minutes, then reduce the oven temperature to 170°C (150°C fan oven) mark 3 and roast for a further 3½ hours.

6 Roll the rashers of bacon into neat rolls. Twist the chipolatas in two to make cocktail sausages and snip with scissors. Take the turkey out of the oven and increase the temperature to 200℃ (180℃ fan oven) mark 6. Pull off the foil and baste the turkey with the juices. Put the bacon rolls and chipolatas around the turkey, then roast for 40 minutes more, basting halfway through.

7 To check whether the turkey is cooked, pierce the thickest part of the flesh with a skewer; the juices should run clear. If there is any sign of blood, return the turkey to the oven for a further 10 minutes, then check again in the same way.

8 Tip the juices out of the turkey into the roasting tin, then lift the turkey, bacon and sausages on to a warm platter. Cover with foil and leave in a warm place for 30 minutes while you make the gravy. To garnish, stuff the turkey cavity with a bunch of mixed herbs. Serve with the cranberry and bread sauces.

Chestnut and Butternut Squash Stuffing

- ½ tbsp olive oil
- 10g (¼oz) butter
- ½ onion, finely chopped
- ½ small butternut squash, peeled and finely chopped
- 1 rosemary sprig, finely chopped
- 1 celery stick, finely chopped

How to cook

1 Heat the oil and butter in a pan and gently fry the onion for 10 minutes. Add the squash and rosemary and continue to cook for another 5 minutes or until everything is soft and golden. Add the celery and pear and cook for 1–2 minutes.

- [ ] 1 small firm pear, finely chopped
- [ ] 100g (3oz) peeled and cooked (or vacuum-packed) chestnuts, roughly chopped
- [ ] 1 slice – about 50g (2oz) – walnut bread, cut into small cubes
- [ ] salt and ground black pepper

Red Wine Gravy

- [ ] juices from the roasted bird
- [ ] 1 tbsp plain flour
- [ ] 150ml (¼ pint) red wine
- [ ] about 1.4 litres (2½ pints) **Giblet Stock** (*see page 25*)
- [ ] 1 tbsp fine shred marmalade

How to cook

2 Add the chestnuts, season with salt and pepper and mix well. Add the bread, mix everything together, then set aside to cool. Cover and chill (overnight if possible).

1 Pour off all but 2 tbsp fat from the roasting tin. Put the roasting tin on the hob over a low heat.

2 Stir in the flour using a wooden spoon, scraping up the juices from the base of the tin, and cook for 2 minutes, stirring constantly.

3 Add the wine, continue to stir, then gradually add the stock. Bring to the boil, then add the marmalade and simmer for 5–10 minutes until thick and syrupy.

Crispy Roast Potatoes

shopping list

- ☐ 1.8kg (4lb) potatoes, preferably King Edward, cut into two-bite pieces
- ☐ 2 tsp paprika
- ☐ 2–3 tbsp goose or white vegetable fat
- ☐ salt

Serves 8

Preparation Time
20 minutes

Cooking Time
1 hour 50 minutes

How to cook

1 Put the potatoes in a pan of salted cold water. Cover and bring to the boil. Boil for 7 minutes, then drain well in a colander.

2 Sprinkle the paprika over the potatoes in the colander, then cover and shake the potatoes roughly, so they become fluffy around the edges.

3 Preheat the oven to 220°C (200°C fan oven) mark 7. Heat the fat in a large roasting tin on the hob. When it sizzles, add the potatoes. Tilt the pan to coat them, taking care as the fat will splatter. Roast in the oven for 1 hour.

4 Reduce the oven temperature to 200°C (180°C fan oven) mark 6 and roast for a further 40 minutes. Shake the potatoes only once or twice during cooking, otherwise the edges won't crisp and brown. Season with a little salt before serving.

Nut and Cranberry Terrine

shopping list

- 125g (4oz) long-grain rice
- 4 tbsp olive oil
- 1 onion, finely chopped
- 1 leek, trimmed and thinly sliced
- 4 celery sticks, thinly sliced
- 4 tbsp chopped mixed fresh herbs, such as sage, parsley and thyme

Serves 8

Preparation Time
45 minutes,
plus cooling

Cooking Time
1 hour 10 minutes

- 40g (1½oz) walnuts, toasted and roughly ground
- 125g (4oz) dolcelatte cheese, crumbled
- 1 large egg, beaten
- 40g (1½oz) fresh white breadcrumbs
- 125g (4oz) fromage frais or crème fraîche
- salt and ground black pepper
- bay leaves to garnish

continued on next page

How to cook

1 Cook the rice for 10 minutes or until just tender. Refresh under cold water, drain thoroughly and set aside. Heat the oil in a frying pan, add the onion, leek, celery and herbs and fry gently for 10 minutes until softened. Transfer to a bowl. Add the rice, walnuts, cheese, egg, breadcrumbs and fromage frais or crème fraîche. Season well and stir to combine.

2 Preheat the oven to 220°C (200°C fan oven) mark 7. Roll out the pastry to a 25.5 x 20.5cm (10 x 8in) rectangle and use to line a 900g (2lb) loaf tin,

pressing the dough into the corners. Trim the overhanging pastry and reserve.

3 Spoon the rice mixture into the pastry case and smooth the surface. Divide the pastry trimmings in half, roll each piece into a long thin rope and twist the two ropes together. Dampen the pastry edges and top with the pastry twist, pressing down gently. Cook the terrine in the oven for 45–50 minutes until golden and a skewer inserted into the centre comes out hot. Remove and leave to cool.

For the topping
- [ ] 125g (4oz) redcurrant jelly
- [ ] 1 tsp lemon juice
- [ ] 125g (4oz) cranberries or
  redcurrants, thawed if frozen

4 To make the topping, heat the redcurrant jelly in a small pan with the lemon juice and 1 tbsp water until melted, then simmer for 3 minutes. Remove from the heat and stir in the fruit.

5 To unmould the pie, turn the loaf tin upside-down and tap gently. Spoon the topping over and leave to set. When cold, garnish with bay leaves.

Hot Water Crust Pastry

- ☐ 225g (8oz) plain flour
- ☐ pinch of salt
- ☐ 50g (2oz) white vegetable fat
- ☐ 100ml (3½fl oz) water

Cranberry Sauce

- ☐ 225g (8oz) fresh cranberries
- ☐ grated zest and juice of 1 orange
- ☐ 4 tbsp fine shred marmalade
- ☐ 125g (4oz) light muscovado sugar
- ☐ 50ml (2fl oz) port

How to cook

1 Sift the flour and salt into a bowl and make a well in the middle. Heat the fat and water in a pan until it comes to the boil. Pour into the flour and work together, using a wooden spoon.

2 When cool enough to handle, knead lightly until smooth; use while still warm and pliable.

How to cook

1 Put the cranberries in a pan. Add the orange zest and juice, marmalade, sugar and port. Mix together, then bring to the boil and simmer for 5–10 minutes, stirring occasionally, until thickened. Tip into a freezerproof container, cool and freeze for up to one month. Defrost thoroughly before use.

Roasted Salmon

shopping list

- 3 lemons, 2 sliced and the juice of ½, plus extra lemon slices to garnish
- 2 salmon sides, filleted, each 1.4kg (3lb), skin on, boned and trimmed
- 2 tbsp dry white wine
- salt and ground black pepper

Serves 20

Preparation Time
20 minutes, plus cooling and chilling

Cooking Time
about 30 minutes

- cucumber slices and 2 large bunches of watercress to garnish

For the dressing
- 500g carton crème fraîche
- 500g carton natural yogurt
- 2 tbsp horseradish sauce
- 3 tbsp freshly chopped tarragon
- 4 tbsp capers, roughly chopped, plus extra to garnish
- ¼ cucumber, seeded and finely chopped

How to cook

1 Preheat the oven to 190°C (170°C fan oven) mark 5. Take two pieces of foil, each large enough to wrap one side of salmon, and put a piece of greaseproof paper on top. Divide the lemon slices between each piece of greaseproof paper and lay the salmon on top, skin side up. Season with salt and pepper, then pour over the lemon juice and wine.

2 Score the skin of each salmon fillet at 4cm (1½in) intervals to mark 10 portions. Scrunch the foil around each fillet, keeping it loose so the fish doesn't stick.

Cook for 25 minutes until the flesh is just opaque. Unwrap the foil and cook for a further 5 minutes until the skin is crisp. Leave the fish to cool quickly in a cold place. Re-wrap and chill.

3 Put all the dressing ingredients in a bowl and season with salt and pepper. Mix well, then cover and chill.

4 Serve the salmon on a platter garnished with lemon, cucumber and watercress. Garnish the dressing with capers and chopped cucumber.

Quick Salmon Mousse

Shopping list

- 300g (11oz) skinless salmon fillet, roughly chopped
- 300g (11oz) ricotta or other soft cheese
- juice of ½ large lemon
- 3 tbsp freshly chopped chives
- 2 large fennel bulbs, thinly sliced

Serves 8

Preparation Time
20 minutes,
plus cooling

- 2 large avocados, sliced
- 2 small courgettes, pared into strips with a vegetable peeler
- 10 tbsp vinaigrette dressing
- 125g (4oz) mixed salad leaves
- 8 slices toasted walnut bread
- 8 slices smoked salmon
- salt and ground black pepper
- lemon wedges to garnish

How to cook

1 Put the salmon in a heatproof bowl and pour over enough boiling water to cover. Cover with clingfilm and leave to cool.

2 Drain the salmon and mash it into the cheese. Add the lemon juice and chives, and season well with salt and pepper. Mix well, then cover and chill for up to one day.

3 Put the fennel, avocado and courgette in a shallow dish and spoon over the vinaigrette dressing.

4 Arrange the fennel, avocado and courgette on eight plates with the salad leaves. Put a slice of bread on each plate, then top with a mound of the salmon mixture and a fold of smoked salmon. Garnish with lemon wedges and serve immediately.

Roasted Vegetable Tartlets

shopping list

- 375g pack ready-rolled puff pastry, thawed if frozen
- plain flour to dust
- 1 medium egg, beaten
- 2 tbsp coarse sea salt
- 300g (11oz) vegetable antipasti in olive oil

Makes 6

Preparation Time
15 minutes

Cooking Time
about 7 minutes

- olive oil, if needed
- 2 tbsp balsamic vinegar
- 190g tub red pepper hummus
- 50g (2oz) wild rocket
- salt and ground black pepper

How to cook

1 Preheat the oven to 220℃ (200℃ fan oven) mark 7. Unroll the puff pastry on a lightly floured surface and cut it into six squares. Put the pastry squares on a large baking sheet and prick each one all over with a fork. Brush the surface with beaten egg and sprinkle the edges with sea salt. Bake for 5–7 minutes or until the pastry is golden brown and cooked through.

2 Pour 4 tbsp of olive oil from the jar of antipasti into a bowl (top it up with a little more olive oil if there's not enough in the antipasti jar). Add the balsamic vinegar, season with salt and pepper, mix well, then set aside.

3 To serve, divide the hummus among the six pastry bases and spread it over the surface. Put the bases on individual plates and spoon over the antipasti – there's no need to be neat. Whisk the balsamic vinegar dressing together. Add the rocket leaves and toss to coat, then pile a small handful of leaves on top of each tartlet. Serve immediately.

Winter Coleslaw

Shopping list

- 4 oranges
- 400g can chickpeas, drained and rinsed
- 450g (1lb) carrots, coarsely grated
- ½ red cabbage, about 550g (1¼lb), finely shredded
- 75g (3oz) sultanas

Serves 6

Preparation Time
15 minutes

- 6 tbsp freshly chopped coriander
- 4 tbsp extra virgin olive oil
- 3 tbsp red wine vinegar
- salt and ground black pepper

How to make

1 Using a sharp knife, cut a thin slice of peel and pith from each end of the oranges. Put the oranges, cut side down, on a board and cut off the peel and pith. Remove any remaining pith. Cut out each segment, leaving the membrane behind. Squeeze the juice from the membrane into a bowl.

2 Put the orange segments and juice in a serving bowl with the chickpeas, carrots, cabbage, sultanas and coriander. Add the oil and vinegar, and season well with salt and pepper.

3 Toss everything together to coat thoroughly. Store the coleslaw in a sealable container in the refrigerator for up to two days.

Stuffed Roast Goose

Shopping list

☐ 5kg (11lb) goose (with giblets for stock)
☐ **Wild Rice and Cranberry Stuffing**
  (see page 24)
☐ 3 red-skinned apples
☐ 4 sprigs of fresh sage, plus extra to garnish

Serves 6

Preparation Time
45 minutes

Cooking Time
about 3 hours, plus
20 minutes resting

- 25g (1oz) butter
- 2 tbsp golden caster sugar
- salt and ground black pepper

For the gravy
- 2 tbsp plain flour
- 150ml (¼ pint) red wine
- 600ml (1 pint) Giblet Stock
  (see page 25)
- 2 tbsp redcurrant jelly

How to cook

1 To make the goose easier to carve, remove the wishbone from the neck by lifting the flap and cutting around the bone with a small knife. Using your fingers, ease the skin away from the flesh to make room for the stuffing, then put the goose on to a tray in the sink and pour a generous amount of freshly-boiled water over it. Pat it dry with kitchen paper.

2 Preheat the oven to 230°C (210°C fan oven) mark 8. Pack the neck of the goose with half of the stuffing and secure the neck shut with skewers or by using a trussing needle with fine string. Put any remaining stuffing on to

a buttered sheet of foil and wrap it up. Season the cavity of the bird with salt and pepper, then put in one whole apple and four sprigs of sage.

3 Put the goose on to a rack in a roasting tin and season well with salt and pepper. Roast for 30 minutes, basting occasionally, then remove and reserve any excess fat. Turn the oven down to 190°C (170°C fan oven) mark 5 and cook for a further 2½ hours, removing excess fat every 20 minutes. 30 minutes before the end of the cooking time, put the parcel of stuffing into the oven.

23

4 Test whether the goose is cooked by piercing the thigh with a thin skewer: the juices should run clear. Remove the goose from the oven and put it on a board. Cover with foil and leave to rest for at least 20 minutes.

5 Meanwhile, cut the remaining apples into thick wedges. Heat the butter in a heavy-based frying pan until it's no longer foaming. Add the apples and the sugar and stir-fry over a high heat for 4–5 minutes until caramelised, then put to one side.

6 To make the gravy, drain all but 3 tbsp fat from the roasting tin. Add the flour and stir to make a smooth paste. Add the wine and boil for 5 minutes, then add the stock and redcurrant jelly and mix well. Bring to the boil and simmer for 5 minutes. Strain before serving. Garnish the goose with sage, and serve with the stuffing and apples.

Wild Rice and Cranberry Stuffing

- 125g (4oz) wild rice
- 225g (8oz) streaky bacon, cut into short strips
- 2 medium red onions, about 225g (8oz) total weight, finely chopped

How to cook

1 Put the rice in a pan and cover with 900ml (1½ pints) cold water. Add ¼ tsp salt and bring to the boil. Simmer, partly covered, for 45 minutes or until the rice is cooked. Drain and leave to cool.

2 Heat a large frying pan, add the bacon and dry-fry, turning from time to time, until lightly browned. Remove the bacon with a slotted spoon and transfer to a bowl. (If you have the goose liver, cook it in the same pan for 2–3 minutes, leave to cool, then

- 75g (3oz) dried cranberries
- 1 medium egg, beaten
- salt and ground black pepper

Giblet Stock

- giblets from the bird
- 1 onion, quartered
- 1 carrot, halved
- 1 celery stick, halved
- 6 black peppercorns
- 1 bay leaf

chop it finely and add it to the bacon.) Add the onions to the frying pan and cook over a low heat until soft and translucent. Add the cranberries and cook for 1–2 minutes, then add the mixture to the bacon and leave to cool completely.

3 Add the cooked rice and the egg to the bacon mixture. Season with salt and pepper, then stir thoroughly to combine. Cover and chill (overnight if possible).

How to cook

1 Put the giblets in a large pan. Add the onion, carrot, celery, peppercorns and bay leaf. Pour in 1.4 litres (2½ pints) cold water, cover and bring to the boil.

2 Simmer for 30 minutes–1 hour, skimming occasionally. Strain through a sieve. Cool quickly, put into a sealable container and chill for up to three days. Makes 1.3 litres (2¼ pints).

Duck with Red Onion Marmalade

shopping list

- 4 duck legs with skin,
- 3 garlic cloves, crushed
- 2 tsp freshly chopped thyme
- 1 tsp salt
- 3 bay leaves
- 900ml (1 ½ pints) olive oil

Serves 4

Preparation Time
25 minutes,
plus overnight
marinating

Cooking Time
about 1 hour

- Braised Red Cabbage (*see page 28*) and Crispy Roast Potatoes (*see page 8*) to serve

For the red onion marmalade
- 125g (4oz) butter
- 550g (1¼lb) red onions, sliced
- 125g (4oz) kumquats, halved
- 125ml (4fl oz) sherry or wine vinegar
- 150g (5oz) golden caster sugar
- grated zest and juice of 1 orange
- 300ml (½ pint) red wine
- salt and ground black pepper

How to cook

1 The night before you want to serve this recipe, put the duck legs in a plastic container and rub in the garlic, thyme and salt. Add the bay leaves, then cover and chill overnight. The next day, remove the duck from the refrigerator, rub off excess salt and rinse under cold running water. Pat dry with kitchen paper.

2 Preheat the oven to 170°C (150°C fan oven) mark 3. Heat the olive oil gently in a pan. Pack the prepared duck legs close together in a single layer in a baking dish and pour the oil over, covering the duck completely. Roast in the oven for 45 minutes until the duck is cooked through.

3 To make the onion marmalade, melt the butter in a pan, add the onions, kumquats and vinegar and simmer, covered, for 15–20 minutes until the onions are soft. Add the sugar, turn up the heat and cook for 10 minutes, stirring, to caramelise the onions. Add the orange zest, juice and wine, then cook gently, uncovered, for 20 minutes until all the liquid has evaporated. Season with salt and pepper.

4 Lift the duck out of the oil and pat dry. Heat a large frying pan and cook the duck over a medium heat for 10–15 minutes until golden and crisp. Serve with marmalade, cabbage and potatoes.

Braised Red Cabbage

- 1 tbsp olive oil
- 1 red onion, halved and sliced
- 2 garlic cloves, crushed
- 1 large red cabbage, about 1kg (2¼lb), shredded
- 2 tbsp light muscovado sugar
- 2 tbsp red wine vinegar
- 8 juniper berries
- ¼ tsp ground allspice
- 300ml (½ pint) vegetable stock
- 2 pears, cored and sliced
- salt and ground black pepper
- fresh thyme sprigs

How to cook

1 Heat the oil in a large pan, add the onion and fry for 5 minutes. Add the remaining ingredients, except the pears, and season with salt and pepper. Bring to the boil, then cover and simmer for 30 minutes.

2 Add the pears and cook for a further 15 minutes or until nearly all the liquid has evaporated and the cabbage is tender. Serve hot, garnished with thyme.

Bread Sauce

- 1 onion, quartered
- 4 cloves
- 2 bay leaves
- 600ml (1 pint) milk
- 125g (4oz) fresh white breadcrumbs
- 4 tbsp double cream
- 25g (1oz) butter
- a little freshly grated nutmeg
- salt and ground black pepper

How to cook

1 Stud each onion quarter with a clove, then put in a pan with the bay leaves and milk. Bring to the boil, take off the heat and leave to infuse for 10 minutes.

2 Use a slotted spoon to lift out the onion and bay leaves; discard. Add the breadcrumbs to the pan and bring to the boil, stirring. Simmer for 5–6 minutes.

3 Stir in the cream and butter, then add the nutmeg, salt and pepper. Spoon into a warmed serving dish and keep warm until ready to serve. Alternatively, tip into a freezerproof container, cool and freeze for up to one month. Defrost thoroughly before use.

Brussels Sprouts with Pancetta

shopping list

- 900g (2lb) Brussels sprouts, halved
- 1 tbsp olive oil
- 130g pack pancetta cubes
- 2 shallots, chopped

Serves 8

Preparation Time
5 minutes

Cooking Time
15 minutes

- 250g (9oz) peeled and cooked (or vacuum-packed) chestnuts
- 15g (½oz) butter
- a pinch of freshly grated nutmeg
- salt

How to cook

1 Bring a pan of salted water to the boil, add the Brussels sprouts and blanch for 2 minutes. Drain and briefly refresh under cold water. Drain well.

2 Heat the oil in a pan and fry the pancetta for 3–4 minutes until golden. Add the shallots and stir-fry for about 5 minutes until softened.

3 Add the Brussels sprouts and chestnuts to the pan and stir-fry for another 5 minutes until heated through.

4 Add the butter and nutmeg and toss well. Serve immediately.

Ginger and Honey-glazed Ham

shopping list

- 4.5–6.8kg (10–15lb) unsmoked gammon on the bone
- 2 shallots, halved
- 6 cloves
- 3 bay leaves
- 2 celery sticks, cut into 5cm (2in) pieces
- 2 tbsp English mustard

Serves 10

Preparation Time
45 minutes, plus cooling

Cooking Time
about 5¾ hours

- 5cm (2in) piece fresh root ginger, peeled and thinly sliced
- 225g (8oz) dark brown sugar
- 2 tbsp clear honey
- 8 tbsp brandy or Madeira
- 4 mangoes, chopped into 5cm (2in) chunks
- 1 tsp mixed spice
- 4 cardamom pods, seeds removed and crushed
- ½ tsp ground cinnamon
- 4 tbsp raisins

How to cook

1 Put the gammon in a large pan. Add the shallots, cloves, bay leaves, celery and cold water to cover. Bring to the boil, cover and simmer gently for about 5 hours. Remove any scum with a slotted spoon. Lift the ham out of the pan, discard the vegetables and herbs, and leave to cool.

2 Preheat the oven to 200°C (180°C fan oven) mark 6. Using a sharp knife, cut away the skin to leave a layer of fat. Score a diamond pattern in the fat and put the ham in a roasting tin. Spread with the mustard and tuck the ginger into the fat. Put the sugar, honey and brandy or Madeira in a pan and heat gently until the sugar has dissolved. Brush over the ham.

3 Put the mango, mixed spice, cardamon pods, cinnamon and raisins in a bowl, add any remaining glaze and mix well. Spoon the mixture around the ham. Cook the ham for 30–40 minutes, basting every 10 minutes. Remove the ham from the tin and set aside. Stir the chutney and put it under a preheated grill for 5 minutes to caramelise the mango. Transfer to a dish and serve with the ham.

Chilli Onions with Goat's Cheese

Shopping list

- 75g (3oz) unsalted butter, softened
- 2 medium red chillies, seeded and finely chopped
- 1 tsp crushed dried chillies
- 6 small red onions

Serves 6

Preparation Time
15 minutes

Cooking Time
45 minutes

- 3 x 100g (3½oz) goat's cheese logs, with rind
- salt and ground black pepper
- balsamic vinegar to serve

How to cook

1 Preheat the oven to 200°C (180°C fan oven) mark 6. Put the butter in a small bowl, beat in the fresh and dried chillies and season well with salt and pepper.

2 Cut off the root of one of the onions, sit it on its base, then make several deep cuts in the top to create a star shape, slicing about two-thirds of the way down the onion. Do the same with the other five onions, then divide the chilli butter equally among them, pushing it down into the cuts.

3 Put the onions in a small roasting tin, cover with foil and bake for 40–45 minutes until soft. About 5 minutes before they are ready, slice each goat's cheese in two, leaving the rind intact, then put on a baking sheet and bake for 2–3 minutes. To serve, put each onion on top of a piece of goat's cheese and drizzle with balsamic vinegar.

Fillet of Beef en Croûte

shopping list

- 1–1.4kg (2¼–3lb) trimmed fillet of beef
- 50g (2oz) butter
- 2 shallots, chopped
- 15g (½oz) dried porcini mushrooms, soaked in 100ml (3½fl oz) boiling water
- 2 garlic cloves, chopped

Serves 6

Preparation Time
1 hour, plus soaking and chilling

Cooking Time
about 1 hour 20 minutes, plus standing

- 225g (8oz) flat mushrooms, finely chopped
- 2 tsp chopped fresh thyme, plus extra sprigs to garnish
- 175g (6oz) chicken liver pâté
- 175g (6oz) thinly sliced Parma ham
- 375g ready-rolled puff pastry
- 1 medium egg, beaten
- salt and ground black pepper
- **Red Wine Sauce** (*see page 39*) to serve

How to cook

1 Season the beef with salt and pepper. Melt 25g (1oz) butter in a large frying pan and, when foaming, add the beef and brown it all over for 4–5 minutes. Transfer to a plate and leave to cool.

2 Melt the remaining butter in a pan, add the shallots and cook for 1 minute. Drain the porcini mushrooms, reserving the liquid, and chop them. Add them to the pan with the garlic, the reserved liquid and the fresh mushrooms. Turn up the heat and cook until the liquid has evaporated, then season with salt and pepper and add the thyme. Leave to cool.

3 Put the chicken liver pâté in a bowl and beat until smooth. Add the mushroom mixture and stir well. Spread half the mushroom mixture evenly over one side of the fillet. Lay half the Parma ham on a length of clingfilm, overlapping the slices. Invert the mushroom-topped beef on to the ham. Spread the remaining mushroom mixture on the other side of the beef, then lay the rest of the Parma ham, also overlapping, on top of the mushroom mixture. Wrap the beef in the clingfilm to form a firm sausage shape, and chill for 30 minutes. Preheat the oven to 220°C (200°C fan oven) mark 7.

4 On a lightly floured surface, cut off one-third of the pastry. Roll out to 3mm (⅛in) thick and 2.5cm (1in) larger all round than the beef. Prick all over with a fork. Transfer to a baking sheet and bake for 12–15 minutes until brown and crisp. Leave to cool, then trim to the size of the beef. Remove the clingfilm from the beef, brush with the egg and place it on the cooked pastry.

5 Roll out the remaining pastry to a 25.5 x 30.5cm (10 x 12in) rectangle. Roll over a lattice pastry cutter and gently ease the lattice open. Cover the beef with the lattice, tuck the ends under and seal the edges. Brush with the beaten egg, then cook on a baking sheet for 40 minutes for rare, or 45 minutes for medium.

6 Leave the beef to stand for 10 minutes before carving. Garnish with thyme and serve with red wine sauce.

Red Wine Sauce

- 350g (12oz) shallots, finely chopped
- 2 tbsp olive oil
- 3 garlic cloves, chopped
- 3 tbsp tomato purée
- 2 tbsp balsamic vinegar
- 200ml (7fl oz) red wine
- 600ml (1 pint) beef stock

How to cook

1 Soften the shallots in the oil for 5 minutes. Add the garlic and tomato purée and cook for 1 minute, then add the balsamic vinegar.

2 Simmer briskly until reduced to almost nothing, then add the red wine and reduce by half. Pour in the beef stock and simmer until reduced by one-third.

Christmas Pudding

shopping list

- 200g (7oz) currants
- 200g (7oz) sultanas
- 200g (7oz) raisins
- 75g (3oz) dried cranberries or cherries
- grated zest and juice of 1 orange
- 50ml (2fl oz) rum
- 50ml (2fl oz) brandy

Serves 12

Preparation Time
20 minutes,
plus soaking

Cooking Time
6 hours

- 1–2 tsp Angostura bitters
- 175g (6oz) fresh breadcrumbs
- 1 small apple, grated
- 1 carrot, grated
- 100g (3½oz) plain flour, sifted
- 1 tsp mixed spice

- 175g (6oz) light vegetarian suet
- 100g (3½oz) dark muscovado sugar
- 50g (2oz) blanched almonds, roughly chopped
- 2 medium eggs

continued on next page

How to cook

1 Put the dried fruit, orange zest and juice in a large bowl. Pour over the rum, brandy and Angostura bitters. Cover and leave to soak in a cool place for at least 1 hour or overnight.

2 Add the breadcrumbs, apple, carrot, flour, mixed spice, suet, sugar, almonds and eggs to the bowl of soaked fruit. Use a wooden spoon to mix everything together well. Now's the time to make a wish!

3 Grease a 1.8 litre (3¼ pint) pudding basin and line with a 60cm (24in) square piece of muslin. Spoon the mixture into the prepared pudding basin and flatten the surface. Gather the muslin up and over the top, then twist and secure with string.

4 Put the basin on an upturned heatproof saucer or trivet in the base of a large pan. Pour in enough boiling water to come halfway up the side of the basin. Cover with a tight-fitting lid and simmer for 6 hours. Keep the water topped up. Remove the basin from the pan and leave to cool. When the pudding is cold, remove it from the basin, then wrap it in clingfilm and a double layer of foil. Store in a cool, dry place for up to six months.

Brandy Butter

- butter to grease
- fresh or frozen cranberries (thawed if frozen), fresh bay leaves and icing sugar to decorate
- **Brandy Butter, Boozy Cream** or **Muscovado Butter** (*see page 42–3*) to serve

- 125g (4oz) unsalted butter
- 125g (4oz) light muscovado sugar, sieved
- 6 tbsp brandy

How to make

5 To reheat, steam for 2½ hours; check the water level every 40 minutes and top up if necessary. Leave the pudding in the pan, covered, to keep warm until needed. Decorate with cranberries and bay leaves, dust with icing sugar. Serve with Brandy Butter, Boozy Cream or Muscovado Butter.

1 Put the butter in a bowl and beat until very soft. Gradually beat in the sugar until very light and fluffy.

2 Beat in the brandy, a spoonful at a time. Cover and chill for at least 3 hours.

Boozy Cream

- 125g (4oz) chopped dried fruit
- 125ml (4fl oz) crème de cacao or Grand Marnier
- 568ml carton double cream
- 100ml (3½fl oz) brandy
- pinch of freshly grated nutmeg
- about 1tbsp golden icing sugar

How to make

1 Put the fruit in a bowl, add the crème de cacao or Grand Marnier and soak for 10 minutes.

2 Lightly whip the cream in a large bowl until thickened. Fold in the brandy, nutmeg, fruit and juices and a little icing sugar to taste. Transfer to a serving bowl and chill until ready to serve.

Muscovado Butter

- 250g (9oz) unsalted butter
- 225g (8oz) light muscovado sugar
- 8tbsp Grand Marnier or Cointreau

How to make

1 Put the butter in a large bowl and add the sugar. Using an electric hand whisk, cream together until smooth and pale.

2 Add the Grand Marnier or Cointreau, a little at a time, continue to whisk for about 5 minutes, until thick and mousse-like. Transfer to a bowl and chill until needed.

Drunken Pears

shopping list

- 4 Williams or Comice pears
- 150g (5oz) granulated sugar
- 300ml (½ pint) red wine
- 150ml (¼ pint) sloe gin
- 1 cinnamon stick

Serves 4

Preparation Time
15 minutes

Cooking Time
50 minutes

- zest of 1 orange
- 6 star anise
- Greek yogurt or whipped cream to serve (optional)

How to cook

1 Peel the pears, cut out the calyx at the base of each and leave the stalks intact. Put the sugar, wine, sloe gin and 300ml (½ pint) water in a small pan and heat gently until the sugar dissolves.

2 Bring to the boil and add the cinnamon stick, orange zest and star anise. Add the pears, then cover and poach over a low heat for 30 minutes or until tender.

3 Remove the pears with a slotted spoon, then continue to heat the liquid until it has reduced to about 200ml (7fl oz) or until syrupy. Pour the syrup over the pears. Serve warm or chilled with Greek yogurt or whipped cream.

Christmas Cake

shopping list

- 1kg (2¼lb) mixed dried fruit
- 100g (3½oz) ready-to-eat pitted prunes, roughly chopped
- 50g (2oz) ready-to-eat dried figs, roughly chopped
- 100g (3½oz) dried cranberries
- grated zest and juice of 1 orange

Serves 16

Preparation Time
30 minutes

Cooking Time
2½ hours, plus cooling

- 2 balls preserved stem ginger in syrup, grated and syrup reserved
- 175ml (6fl oz) brandy
- 2 splashes Angostura bitters
- 175g (6oz) unsalted butter, cubed, plus extra to grease

- 175g (6oz) dark muscovado sugar
- 200g (7oz) self-raising flour
- ½ tsp ground cinnamon
- ½ tsp freshly grated nutmeg
- ½ tsp ground cloves
- 4 medium eggs, beaten

How to cook

1 Preheat the oven to 150°C (130°C fan oven) mark 2. Grease and line the base and sides of a 20.5cm (8in) round, deep cake tin with greaseproof paper.

2 Put all the dried fruit in a very large pan and add the ginger, 1 tbsp reserved ginger syrup, orange zest and juice, brandy and Angostura bitters. Bring to the boil, then simmer for 5 minutes. Add the butter and sugar and heat gently to melt. Stir occasionally until the sugar dissolves.

3 Take the pan off the heat and leave to cool for a couple of minutes. Add the flour, spices and beaten egg and mix well. Pour the mixture into the prepared tin and level the top. Wrap the outside of the tin in brown paper and secure with string to protect the cake during cooking. Bake for 2–2½ hours until the cake is firm to the touch. Test by inserting a skewer into the centre of the cake – it should come out clean.

4 Leave the cake to cool in the tin for 2–3 hours, then remove from the tin, leaving the greaseproof paper on, and leave to cool completely on a wire rack. Wrap the cake in a layer of clingfilm, then in foil. Store in an airtight container for up to three months.

Mince Pies

Makes 24

Preparation Time
15 minutes, plus chilling

Cooking Time
12–15 minutes

- finely grated zest of 1 orange
- 1 egg, beaten
- 400g jar mincemeat
- icing sugar to dust

How to cook

1 Put the flour in a food processor. Add the butter, cream cheese, egg yolk and orange zest and whiz until the mixture just comes together. Tip the mixture into a large bowl and bring the dough together with your hands. Shape into a ball, wrap in clingfilm and put in the freezer for 5 minutes.

2 Preheat the oven to 220°C (200°C fan) mark 7. Cut off about one-third of the pastry dough and set aside. Roll out the remainder on a lightly floured worksurface to 5mm (¼in) thick. Stamp out circles with a 6.5cm (2½in) cutter to make 24 rounds, re-rolling the dough as necessary. Use the pastry circles to line two 12-hole patty tins. Roll out the reserved pastry and use a star cutter to stamp out the stars.

3 Put 1 tsp mincemeat into each pastry case, then top with pastry stars. Brush the tops with beaten egg, then bake for 12–15 minutes until golden. Remove from the tins and leave to cool on a wire rack. Serve warm or cold, dusted with icing sugar. Store in an airtight container for up to four days.

Chocolate Mousse Roulade

shopping list

- 6 large eggs, separated
- 150g (5oz) caster sugar, plus extra to sprinkle
- 50g (2oz) cocoa powder
- frosted fruit and leaves to decorate

Serves 8

Preparation Time
45 minutes, plus
2 hours chilling

Cooking Time
40 minutes,
plus cooling

For the filling
- 225g (8oz) milk chocolate, roughly chopped
- 2 large eggs, separated
- 125g (4oz) fresh or frozen cranberries, halved
- 50g (2oz) granulated sugar
- grated zest and juice of ½ medium orange
- 200ml (7fl oz) double cream
- **Frosted Fruit and Leaves** or **Nut Praline** to serve *(see page 53)*

How to cook

1 Preheat the oven to 180°C (160°C fan oven) mark 4. Line a 30.5 x 20.5cm (12 x 8in) Swiss roll tin with non-stick baking parchment – it needs to stick up around the edges of the tin by 5cm (2in) to allow the cake to rise.

2 First, make the filling. Put the chocolate in a large heatproof bowl and add 50ml (2fl oz) water. Place over a pan of gently simmering water, making sure the bowl doesn't touch the water. Leave to melt for 15–20 minutes. Remove the bowl from the heat and, without stirring, add the egg yolks, then stir until smooth. In a separate, grease-free bowl, whisk the egg whites until soft peaks form, then fold into the chocolate. Cover and chill for at least 2 hours.

3 Put the cranberries in a pan with the sugar, orange zest and juice, and 100ml (3½fl oz) water. Bring to a gentle simmer, then leave to barely simmer for 30 minutes, stirring occasionally until the cranberries are soft; there should be no excess liquid left in the pan. Remove from the heat and leave to cool.

4 To make the cake, put the egg yolks in a bowl and whisk with an electric hand whisk for 1–2 minutes until pale. Add the sugar and whisk until the mixture has the consistency of thick cream. Sift the cocoa powder over the mixture and fold in with a large metal spoon. In a separate, grease-free bowl, whisk the egg whites until soft peaks form. Stir a spoonful of the egg whites into the chocolate mixture to loosen it, then fold in the remainder. Pour the mixture into the prepared tin and bake for about 25 minutes or until well risen and spongy. Leave to cool completely in the tin (it will sink dramatically).

5 When the cake is cold, put a sheet of baking parchment on the worksurface and sprinkle with caster sugar. Turn the cake out on to the sugar and peel off the parchment. Spoon the chocolate filling on top and spread to within 2.5cm (1in) of the edge. Sprinkle over the glazed cranberries. Lightly whip the cream, then spread lightly over the cranberries to cover.

6 Holding a short edge of the baking parchment, gently lift and roll, pushing the edge down so it starts to curl. Keep lifting and rolling as the cake comes away from the paper. Don't worry if it cracks. Remove the paper. Chill for up to 8 hours. Decorate with the frosted fruit and leaves or nut praline.

Frosted Fruit and Leaves

- fresh cranberries or redcurrants
- fresh bay or holly leaves
- 1 medium egg white, lightly beaten
- 25g (1oz) caster sugar

How to make

1 Brush the berries and leaves lightly with beaten egg white.

2 Spread the sugar on a tray, making sure there are no lumps. Dip the berries and leaves into the sugar, shake off any excess, then leave to dry on a tray lined with greaseproof paper or baking parchment for about 1 hour.

Nut Praline

- 250g (9oz) golden caster sugar
- 175g (6oz) nuts

How to cook

1 Line a baking sheet with baking parchment and fill a bowl with very cold water. Put the sugar in a heavy-based pan over a low heat. Shake the pan gently to dissolve the sugar.

2 When the sugar has turned a dark golden brown colour, pour in the nuts and stir once with a wooden spoon.

3 Dip the base of the pan into cold water to prevent the praline from burning, then quickly pour the praline on to the parchment and spread out. Cool for 20 minutes, then break into pieces with a rolling pin. For fine praline, crush in a food processor.

Nutty Chocolate Truffles

shopping list

- 100g (3½oz) hazelnuts
- 200g (7oz) plain chocolate (minimum 50% cocoa solids), broken into pieces
- 25g (1oz) butter

Makes 30

Preparation Time
20 minutes, plus
½ hours chilling

Cooking Time
12 minutes

- 150ml (¼ pint) double cream
- 3 tbsp cocoa powder, sifted
- 3 tbsp golden icing sugar, sifted

How to cook

1 Put the hazelnuts in a frying pan and heat gently for 3–4 minutes, shaking the pan occasionally, until toasted all over. Put 30 nuts in a bowl and leave to cool. Whiz the remaining nuts in a food processor until finely chopped. Put the chopped nuts in a shallow dish.

2 Melt the chocolate in a heatproof bowl over a pan of gently simmering water, taking care not to let the bowl touch the water. In a separate pan, melt the butter and cream. Bring just to the boil, then remove from the heat. Carefully stir into the chocolate. Whisk until cool and thick, then chill for 1–2 hours.

3 Put the cocoa powder and icing sugar in separate shallow dishes. Scoop up a teaspoonful of the chilled truffle mixture and push a hazelnut into the centre. Working quickly, shape into a ball, then roll in cocoa powder, icing sugar or chopped nuts. Repeat with the remaining truffle mixture, then chill until ready to serve.

Cookies and Cream Fudge

shopping list

- ☐ sunflower oil to grease
- ☐ 125g (4oz) unsalted butter
- ☐ 200ml (7fl oz) evaporated milk
- ☐ 450g (1lb) golden caster sugar
- ☐ 1 tsp vanilla extract

Makes 36

Preparation Time
10 minutes,
plus cooling and
overnight chilling

Cooking Time
15 minutes

- 75g (3oz) plain chocolate, chopped
- 25g (1oz) hazelnuts, toasted and roughly chopped
- 6 bourbon biscuits or Oreo cookies, roughly chopped

How to cook

1 Lightly grease a 450g (1lb) loaf tin. Put the butter, evaporated milk, sugar, vanilla extract and 50ml (2fl oz) water in a large heavy-based pan, set over a low heat and stir until the butter has melted and the sugar dissolved. Increase the heat and boil gently for about 10 minutes, stirring all the time, until the mixture forms a soft ball when ½tsp is dropped into a cup of cold water. Remove the pan from the heat and, working quickly, divide the fudge mixture between two bowls. Add the chocolate to one of the bowls, and allow it to melt into the fudge. Stir the mixture gently until smooth.

2 Pour half the chocolate fudge into the tin and smooth the surface, then scatter over half the hazelnuts and half the biscuits.

3 Pour the vanilla fudge into the tin, then top with the remaining nuts and biscuits. Finish with a layer of the chocolate fudge and set aside to cool. Cover with clingfilm and chill overnight. Cut the fudge into slices, then chop into 36 pieces.

Mulled Wine

shopping list

- 2 oranges
- 6 cloves
- 75cl bottle fruity red wine
- 2 measures (50ml) brandy or Cointreau

Serves 6

Preparation Time
10 minutes,
plus infusing

Cooking Time
10–15 minutes

- 1 cinnamon stick, broken
- ½ tsp mixed spice
- 2 tbsp golden granulated sugar

How to cook

1 Cut one of the oranges into six wedges and push a clove into each wedge. Using a vegetable peeler, carefully pare the zest of the other orange into strips.

2 Put the clove-studded orange wedges in a stainless-steel pan, along with the red wine, brandy or Cointreau, cinnamon stick, mixed spice and sugar. Warm gently over a low heat for 10–15 minutes, then remove the pan from the heat and set aside for 10 minutes to let the flavours infuse.

3 Strain the wine into a serving jug through a non-metallic sieve to remove the orange wedges and the cinnamon. Serve in heatproof glasses with a strip of orange zest draped over each glass.

Fruity Punch

shopping list

- [ ] 1 litre (1¾ pints) apple juice, chilled
- [ ] 1 litre (1¾ pints) ginger ale, chilled
- [ ] 2 apples, sliced and cut into stars, or star fruit, thinly sliced

Serves 8

Preparation Time
5 minutes

How to make

1 Put the apple juice, ginger ale and star-shaped fruit in a large bowl and mix well.

2 Pour into a large jug and serve.

Champagne Cocktail

shopping list

- 125ml (4fl oz) Grand Marnier
- 75ml (2½fl oz) grenadine
- 1 large orange, cut into 8 wedges

Serves 8

Preparation Time
5 minutes

- 8 sugar cubes or sugar sticks
- 75cl bottle champagne, cava or other sparkling wine, chilled

How to make

1 Measure out the Grand Marnier and grenadine and divide among eight champagne glasses. Add an orange wedge and a sugar cube or stick to each glass.

2 Top up the glasses with the champagne, cava or sparkling wine and serve immediately.

Other titles available:

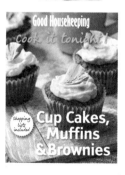

First published in Great Britain in 2009
by Collins & Brown
10 Southcombe Street
London W14 0RA

An imprint of Anova Books Company Ltd
www.anovabooks.com

The Good Housekeeping website is:
www.allaboutyou.com/goodhousekeeping

ISBN 978-1-84340-576-4

The recipes in this book have been chosen
from titles in the Good Housekeeping
Easy to Make! series.

A catalogue record for this book is available
from the British Library.

Reproduction by Dot Gradations Ltd, UK
Printed and bound by Graphicom, Italy

Photography by Nicki Dowey.